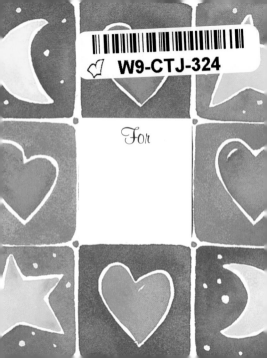

W9-CTJ-324

For

DREAMS CAN COME TRUE

Written and compiled
by Evelyn L. Beilenson

Illustrated by Kathy Davis

Peter Pauper Press, Inc.
WHITE PLAINS, NEW YORK

DReams can Come TRue

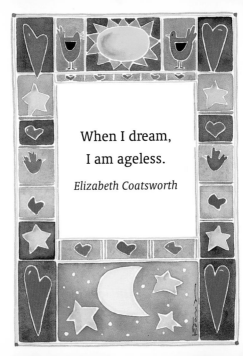

When I dream,
I am ageless.

Elizabeth Coatsworth

Without dreams,
we are rudderless.
Dare to chart your
own course!

Women have to
summon up
courage to fulfill
dormant dreams.

Alice Walker

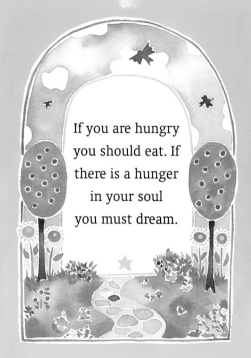

If you are hungry
you should eat. If
there is a hunger
in your soul
you must dream.

I believe that imagination is stronger than knowledge—that myth is more potent than history. I believe that dreams are more powerful than facts.

Robert Fulghum

They who dream by day are cognizant of many things which escape those who dream only by night.

Edgar Allan Poe

A dream not understood

is like a letter not opened.

The Talmud

When it is dark enough,

you can see the stars.

Charles A. Beard

It is difficult to say what is impossible, for the dream of

yesterday is the hope of today and the reality of tomorrow.

Robert H. Goddard

Success is not the result of
spontaneous combustion.

You must set yourself on fire.

Reggie Leach

You do not need a sky full of stars to dream on. Find the one that shines for you.

Some of the best
lessons in life are
learned from dreams
that have failed.

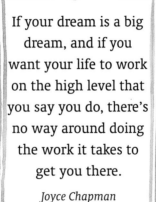

If your dream is a big dream, and if you want your life to work on the high level that you say you do, there's no way around doing the work it takes to get you there.

Joyce Chapman

If one advances in the directions of his dreams, and endeavors to live the life which he has imagined, he will meet with a success unexpected in common hours.

Henry David Thoreau

We compose our own dreams. Each is unique. It belongs entirely to the dreamer, only to be shared by a willing teller with a receptive listener.

Don't be afraid of the
space between your
dreams and reality.
If you can dream it,
you can make it so.

Belva Davis

No one ever gets far unless

he accomplishes the impossible

at least once a day.

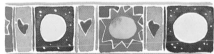

Elbert Hubbard

You see things and you say "Why?";

but I dream things that never were

and I say "Why not?"

George Bernard Shaw

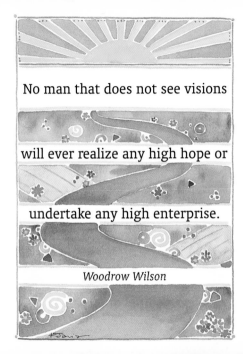

No man that does not see visions

will ever realize any high hope or

undertake any high enterprise.

Woodrow Wilson

All the darkness of the world

cannot put out the light

of one small candle.

Anonymous

Dreams are the keys
to our hearts' desire.
Unlock the door and
make your desires
come true.

To play great
music, you must
keep your eyes on
a distant star.

Yehudi Menuhin

Nothing can stop
the person with
the right attitude
from pursuing
her dreams.

Carry your
dreams with you,
and the world
will be a more
beautiful place.

Dreams pass into
the reality of action.
From the action stems
the dream again; and
this interdependence
produces the highest
form of living.

Anaïs Nin

Rose-colored glasses
are never made
in bifocals. Nobody
wants to read the small
print in dreams.

Ann Landers

What sunshine is to flowers,

dreams are to life.

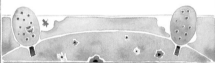

They enrich your very being.

The Possible's slow fuse is lit

By the Imagination.

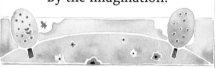

Emily Dickinson

Dreams are renewable. No matter
what our age or condition, there are

still untapped possibilities within us
and new beauty waiting to be born.

Dale Turner

If you have built your castles in the air, your work need not be lost;

that is where they should be. Now put the foundations under them.

Henry David Thoreau

Trust the lessons
of your dreams and
take risks.

Dream while you live
your life and you will
live larger still.

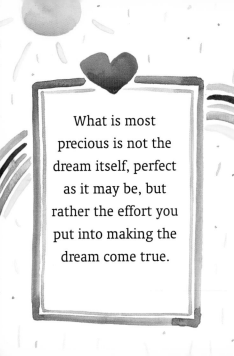

What is most precious is not the dream itself, perfect as it may be, but rather the effort you put into making the dream come true.

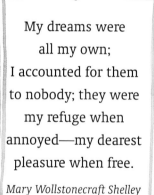

My dreams were
all my own;
I accounted for them
to nobody; they were
my refuge when
annoyed—my dearest
pleasure when free.

Mary Wollstonecraft Shelley

A little sun, a little rain,
  A soft wind blowing
  from the West,
And woods and fields are
sweet again
  And warmth within the
  mountain breast,
A little love, a little trust,

A soft impulse, a
sudden dream,
And life as dry as desert
dust,
Is fresher than a
mountain stream.

Stopford A. Brooke

You can't depend on your

judgment when your imagination

is out of focus.

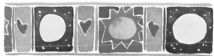

Mark Twain

Like flames, dreams are

difficult to extinguish.

They brighten the path

down life's road.

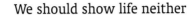

We should show life neither

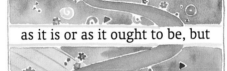

as it is or as it ought to be, but

only as we see it in our dreams.

Tolstoy

Each dream is unique, like each sunrise, with different feelings, textures, and colors.

Fariba Bogzaran

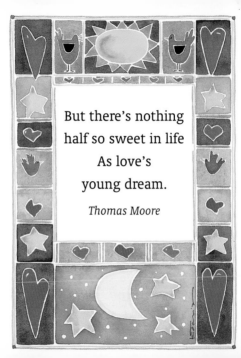

But there's nothing
half so sweet in life
As love's
young dream.

Thomas Moore

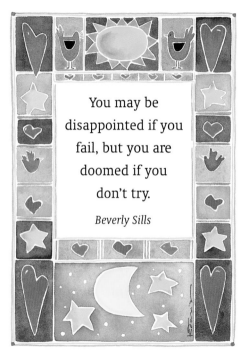

You may be
disappointed if you
fail, but you are
doomed if you
don't try.

Beverly Sills

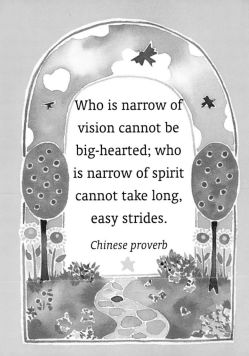

Who is narrow of vision cannot be big-hearted; who is narrow of spirit cannot take long, easy strides.

Chinese proverb

Go forward
and take control
of your dreams.
They are yours
to do with as
you wish.

Maybe you can't dream
the same dreams when
you're 34 that you did
when you were 24, you
know, but you can still
dream something.

Bruce Springsteen

Nobody gets to
live life backward. Look
ahead—that's where
your future lies.

Ann Landers

The successful person

is one who has made

her dreams come true.

The past is the past.

The future is made up

of hopes and dreams.

The future belongs to
those who believe in

the beauty of their dreams.

Eleanor Roosevelt

The human mind is a miracle. Once it accepts a new idea or learns a new fact, it stretches forever and

never goes back to its original dimension. It is limitless.

Leo Buscaglia

Look within
and dream.

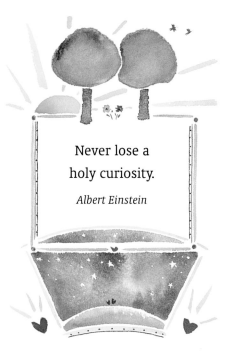

Never lose a
holy curiosity.

Albert Einstein

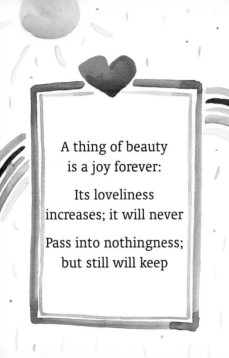

A thing of beauty
is a joy forever:

Its loveliness
increases; it will never

Pass into nothingness;
but still will keep

A bower quiet for us,
and a sleep

Full of sweet dreams
and health,
and quiet breathing.

John Keats

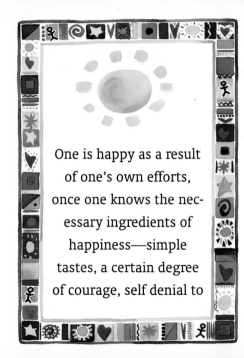

One is happy as a result
of one's own efforts,
once one knows the nec-
essary ingredients of
happiness—simple
tastes, a certain degree
of courage, self denial to

a point, love of work, and, above all, a clear conscience. Happiness is no vague dream, of that I now feel certain.

George Sand

Dream that

there is fulfillment

and fulfillment

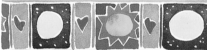

can be attained.

From your

dreams find the

power to energize

your waking life

Without the

inspiration of a

dream, there is

no grand design.

Shelter your dreams.

Only then

can you

possess them.

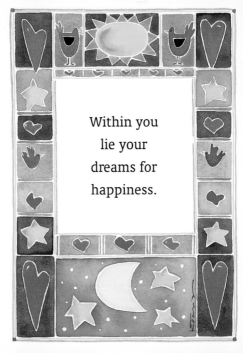

Within you
lie your
dreams for
happiness.

Dreams come
in "can do's,"
failures in
"can't do's."

In your
dreams, nothing
is impossible.

And our dreams
are who we are.

Barbara Sher

We are the music-makers,

And we are the
dreamers of dreams,

Wandering by
lone sea breakers,

And sitting by
desolate streams;

World-losers and
world-forsakers,

On whom the
pale moon gleams:

Yet we are the
movers and shakers

Of the world forever,
it seems.

Arthur William Edgar O'Shaughnessy

Believe in

life's force and

dare to dream.

To keep a lamp burning we

have to keep putting oil in it.

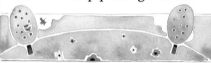

Mother Teresa

The way I see it, if you
want the rainbow, you gotta

put up with the rain.

Dolly Parton

Cherish your visions and your dreams, as they are the children of

your soul; the blueprints of your ultimate achievements.

Napoleon Hill

Invention requires
knowledge, but it is
driven by dreams.

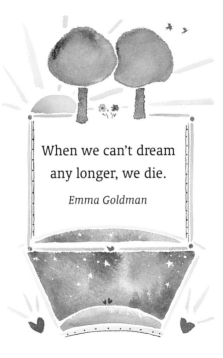

When we can't dream
any longer, we die.

Emma Goldman

I've dreamt in my
life dreams that
have stayed with
me ever after, and
changed my ideas;
they've gone
through and

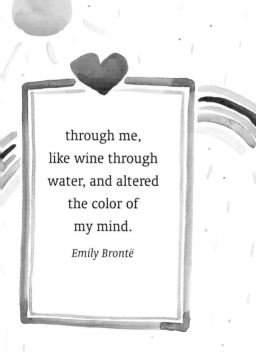

through me,
like wine through
water, and altered
the color of
my mind.

Emily Brontë

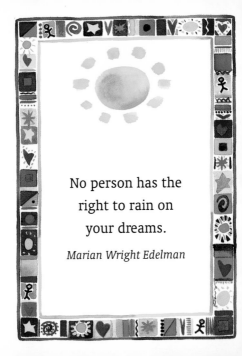

No person has the
right to rain on
your dreams.

Marian Wright Edelman

A dream is a gift you
give to yourself.

Believe in *your* dreams.